BEGINNER'S BOOK OF MODULAR ORIGAMI POLYHEDRA
THE PLATONIC SOLIDS

Rona Gurkewitz

Bennett Arnstein

DOVER PUBLICATIONS, INC.
Mineola, New York

Bibliographical Note

Beginner's Book of Modular Origami Polyhedra: The Platonic Solids is a
new work, first published by Dover Publications, Inc., in 2008.

International Standard Book Number

ISBN-13: 978-0-486-46172-4
ISBN-10: 0-486-46172-6

Manufactured in the United States by Courier Corporation
46172606
www.doverpublications.com

TABLE OF CONTENTS

PLATONIC SOLIDS

Tetrahedron
4 triangle faces
6 edges
4 vertices
dual: tetrahedron

Cube
6 square faces
12 edges
8 vertices
dual: octahedron

Icosahedron
20 triangle faces
30 edges
12 vertices
dual: dodecahedron

Octahedron
8 triangle faces
12 edges
6 vertices
dual: cube

Dodecahedron
12 pentagon faces
30 edges
20 vertices
dual: icosahedron

BACKGROUND

BACKGROUND

1. What is modular origami?

Modular origami is origami made from several sheets of paper that have been folded into modules, also called units. The modules are usually identically folded but may be of several types. The modules are assembled into models that most often are patterned after the 3D geometric shapes called polyhedra.

2. What is the connection between modular origami and polyhedra?

Underlying most 3D modular origami is a uniform, convex polyhedral shape. The modules in the model are in positions corresponding to either the faces, edges or corners (vertices) of the polyhedral shape. Convex polyhedra don't have spikes. Uniform polyhedra have all of their corners having the same arrangement of shapes around them. For example, there are three squares meeting at each corner of a cube. So the more you know about polyhedra, the more modular origami shapes you can make.

3. What is a polyhedron?

A 3D polyhedron is a shape made up of polygons for sides, where a polygon is a shape made up of line segments connected in a row, such as a triangle or a square.

4. What are the Platonic Solids?

The Platonic Solids are five convex polyhedra that have been known since the time of Plato, the cube, the tetrahedron, the octahedron, the dodecahedron and the icosahedron, pictured on p iv. Each of these polyhedra has all of its faces the same regular polygon which means also that all of its edges are the same length. It can be shown that these are the only five geometric shapes with these properties. In addition, their vertices all lie on a sphere.

5. A short history of the relevance of the Platonic Solids

In Plato's times the Platonic solids were equated with the following elements: tetrahedron-fire; cube-earth; octahedron-air; icosahedron-water and dodecahedron-universe. In the 1600s, Johannes Kepler used them as a basis for his system of astronomy. During the Renaissance artists used them as the subject of their art to better understand perspective. Starting in the 1800s polyhedra were used as models for crystal structures. Haeckel in the 1800s drew pictures of radiolaria which have icosahedral shape. In the 20th century virus coats were found to be icosahedral, fullerenes are molecules based on other polyhedral shapes, scientists used nanotechnology to build molecules of polyhedral shapes. Many 20th century artists and sculptors incorporated polyhedra into their work.

2

FURTHER READING

1. Cromwell,Peter; Polyhedra; Cambridge University Press,1997
2. Fuse; Unit Polyhedron Origami,Japan Publications, 2006
3. Fuse; Unit Origami,Japan Publications, 1990
4. Gurkewitz and Arnstein, 3D Geometric Origami: Modular Polyhedra;DoverPublications, 1996
5. Gurkewitz and Arnstein, Multimodular Origami Polyhedra:Archimedeans, Buckyballs and Duality, Dover Publications, 2003
6. Kawamura;Polyhedron Origami for Beginners,Japan Publications, 2002
7. Mitchell; Mathematical Origami; Tarquin Publications,1997
8. Montroll; Constellation of Origami Polyhedra; Dover Publications,2004
9. Montroll; A Plethora of Polyhedra in Origami; Dover Publications,2002
10. Mukerji; Marvelous Modular Origami; AKPeters,2007
11. Simon, Arnstein and Gurkewitz; Modular Origami Polyhedra; Dover Publications, 1999
12. Wenninger, Magnus; Polyhedron Models; Cambridge University Press, 1970

LINKS

Krystyna Burczyk	www1.zetosa.com.pl/burczyk/origami/galery1-en.htm
George Hart	www.georgehart.com/
Tom Hull	www.merrimack.edu/~thull/
David Mitchell	www.origamiheaven.com
Jeannine Mosely	world.std.com/~j9/sponge/
Meenakshi Mukerji	home.comcast.net/~meenaks/origami
Mette Pederson	mette.pederson.com/
David Petty	members.aol.com/ukpetd/
James Plank	www.cs.utk.edu/~plank/plank/origami/origami.html
Francis Ow	web.singnet.com.sg/~owrigami/
Eric Weisstein	mathworld.wolfram.com/origami.html
Magnus Wenninger	employees.csbsju.edu/mwenninger/
Joseph Wu	www.origami.as/home.html

ORIGAMI SOCIETIES

British Origami Society	www.britishorigami.info
Origami-USA	www.origami-usa.org/

MAKING THE MODELS

DEFINITION OF SYMBOLS

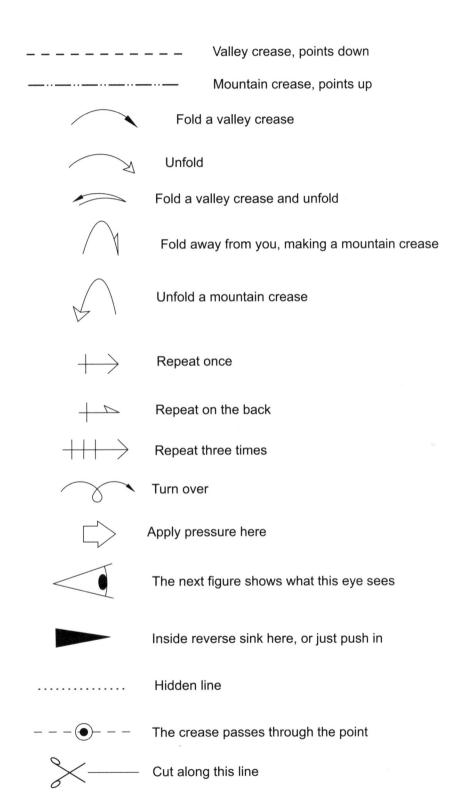

— — — — — — — — — Valley crease, points down

—··—··—·—··—··— Mountain crease, points up

Fold a valley crease

Unfold

Fold a valley crease and unfold

Fold away from you, making a mountain crease

Unfold a mountain crease

Repeat once

Repeat on the back

Repeat three times

Turn over

Apply pressure here

The next figure shows what this eye sees

Inside reverse sink here, or just push in

············· Hidden line

— — —◉— — — The crease passes through the point

Cut along this line

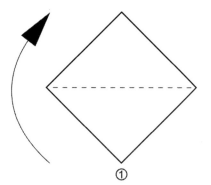

① Start with a square in diamond position. Fold the bottom point to the top point .

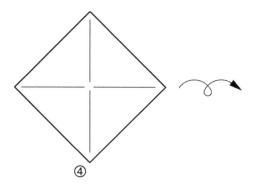

② Unfold.

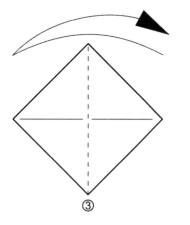

③ Fold the right point to the left point. Unfold.

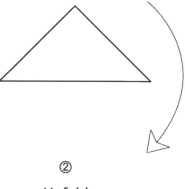

④ Turn the model over.

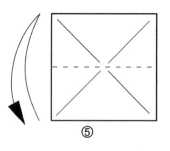

⑤ Fold the bottom edge to the top edge. Unfold.

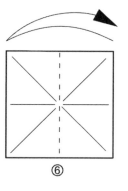

⑥ Fold the right edge to the left edge. Unfold.

6

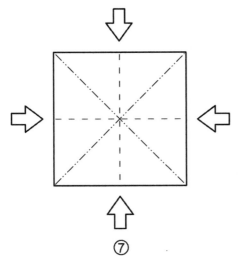

⑦

Push in at the center of each edge.
The model will become three dimen-
sional.

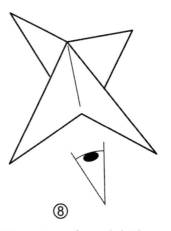

⑧

Top view of model. The next
step is viewed from below.

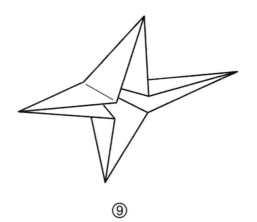

⑨

Bottom view of model.

HOW TO MAKE AN EQUILATERAL TRIANGLE
FROM A SQUARE

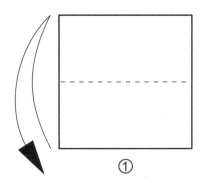

① Fold the bottom edge to the top edge. Unfold.

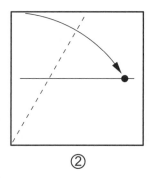

② Fold upper left corner to crease with new crease starting at lower left corner.

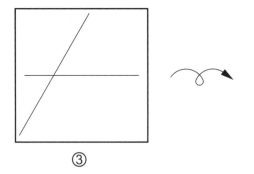

③ Step 2 completed. Turn model over.

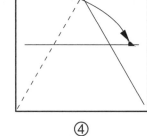

④ Repeat step 2.

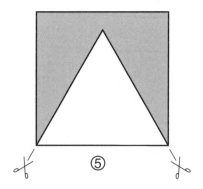

⑤ The equilateral triangle is finished. Cut it out and discard the shaded portion.

HOW TO MAKE AN EQUILATERAL TRIANGLE

FROM A LETTER-SIZE RECTANGLE

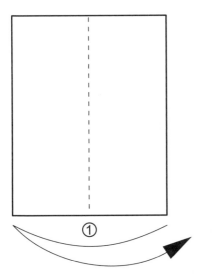

①

Start with short edge on top. Fold right edge to left edge. Unfold.

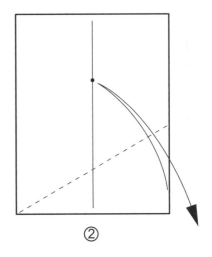

②

Fold lower right corner to center crease with new crease going to lower left corner.

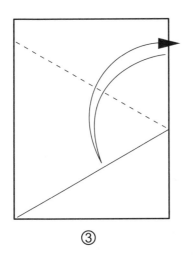

③

Fold right edge to crease made in step 2. Unfold.

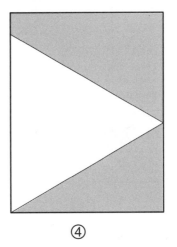

④

One big triangle finished. Cut it out and discard the shaded portion.

HOW TO MAKE AN EQUILATERAL TRIANGLE

SIX HALF-SIZE TRIANGLES FROM A RECTANGLE:

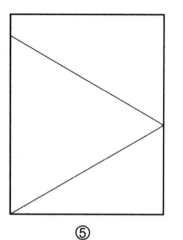

⑤

Start with step 4 of triangle from a letter sized rectangle.

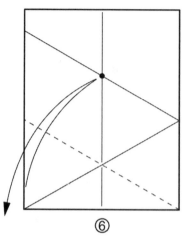

⑥

Fold the lower left corner to the center crease with the new crease going to the lower right corner. Unfold.

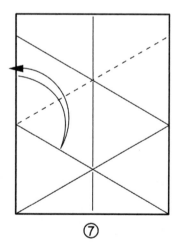

⑦

Fold the upper part of the left edge to the crease made in step 6. Unfold.

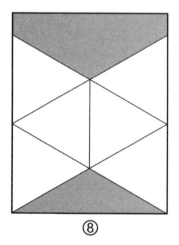

⑧

Six half-size triangles finished. Cut out the triangles and discard the shaded portions.

HOW TO MAKE A HEXAGON
FROM A SQUARE

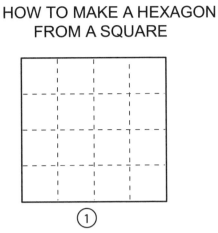

①

Crease a square into four equal spaces, horizontally and vertically.

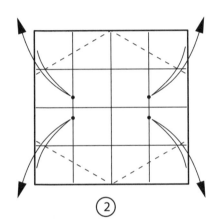

②

Fold each corner to the nearest vertical crease. Unfold.

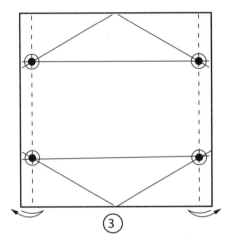

③

Make two creases through the points indicated.

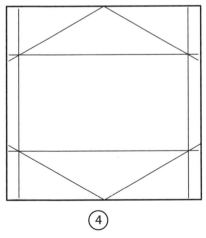

④

Step 3 complete.

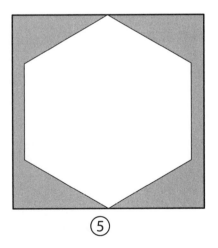

⑤

The hexagon is finished. Cut it out and discard the shaded portion.

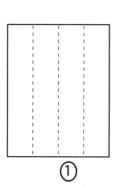

① Crease the rectangle into four equal spaces.

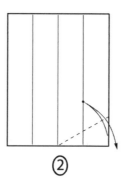

② Fold the lower right corner to the first vertical crease with new crease starting a center of bottom edge. Unfold.

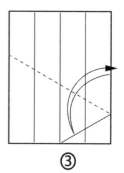

③ Fold right edge to crease from last step. Unfold.

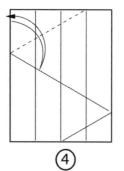

④ Fold top of left edge to crease from last step . Unfold.

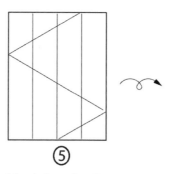

⑤ Model so far. Turn model over.

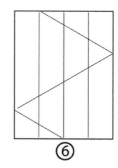

⑥ Repeat steps 2-5 on this side of the paper.

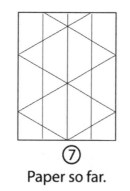

⑦ Paper so far.

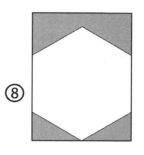

⑧ The hexagon is finished. Cut it out and discard the shaded parts of the paper.

CUBES

THE JACKSON CUBE
by Paul Jackson

Six modules can be assembled to form a cube. The modules are folded from squares. A good color combination is three colors, squares of the same color on opposite sides of the cube.

①

All the modules are folded the same way. Fold the upper edge down to approximately the center of the square. There is no exact location. There is no center crease because it would show on the finished model. See next step for how to estimate the location of the fold.

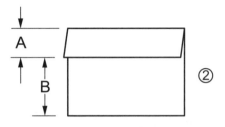

②

Ideally, the width of the folded portion, distance "A", should be half the width of the remaining portion, distance "B". Any distance will be ok though.

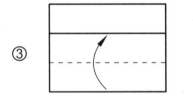

③

Fold the lower edge up to meet the new location of the original upper edge.

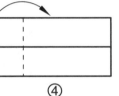

④

There is no exact location for the next crease for the same reason as before. Fold the left edge approximately to the center. See the next step for how to estimate the location of the crease.

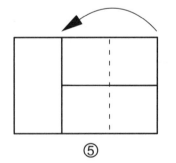

⑤

Estimate the width of the folded portion to be half the width of the unfolded portion; or estimate the unfolded portion to be a square. Fold the right edge up against the original left edge, forming a cupboard-door fold.

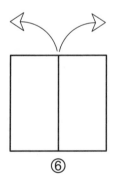

⑥

Unfold the cupboard-doors so they stick straight out from the central portion.

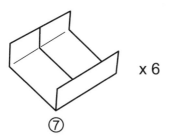

x 6

⑦

The module is finished. Make six, two of each of three colors. Opposite sides of the cube will be the same color.

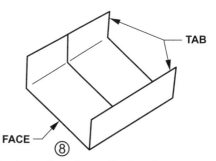

TAB

FACE ⑧

The central portion is called a face. The cupboard-doors are called tabs.

⑨

Start by placing a second-color module face down on a level surface.

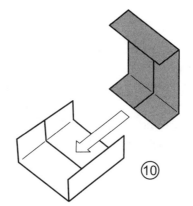

⑩

Insert the bottom tab of a first-color module between the tabs of the second-color module.

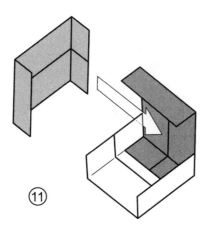

⑪

Insert a third-color module so its face covers the rear tab of the second-color module, and its rear tab goes between the tabs of the first-color module.

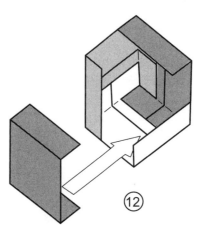

⑫

Insert the other first-color module opposite the existing one, with its bottom tab going between the tabs of the second-color module, and its face covering the left tab of the third-color module.

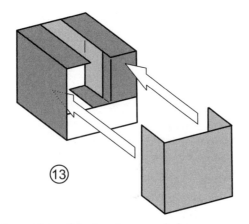

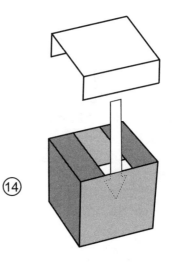

Insert the other third-color module opposite the existing one, with each tab going between the tabs of a first-color module, and its face covering the front tab of the second-color module.

Insert the remaining second-color module so that each tab goes between the tabs of one third-color module, and its face covers the upper tabs of the first-color modules.

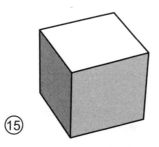

The cube is finished.

SONOBE CUBE
by Mitsunobu Sonobe

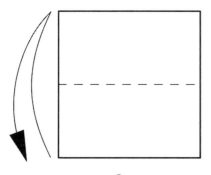

①

Fold bottom edge to
top and unfold

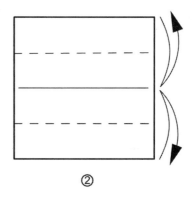

②

Fold bottom and top
edges to center crease
and unfold

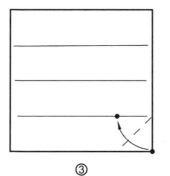

③

Fold bottom right corner
to first horizontal crease
and unfold.

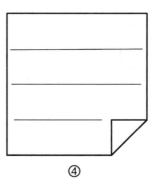

④

Completed fold.

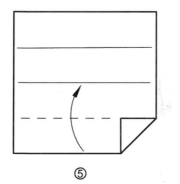

⑤

Fold bottom edge to
center crease.

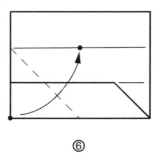

⑥

Fold lower left edge
diagonally to top crease.

SONOBE CUBE

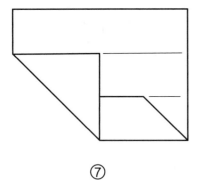

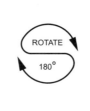

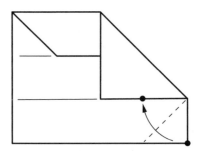

⑦

Completed fold. Rotate.

⑧

Fold lower right corner to first folded edge.

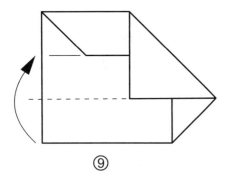

⑨

Fold bottom edge up along the existing crease.

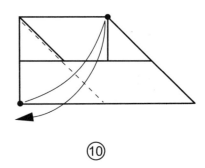

⑩

Fold lower left corner to upper right corner and unfold.

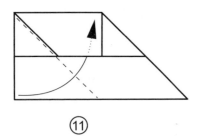

⑪

Refold along the existing crease, slipping the lower left corner under the top layer.

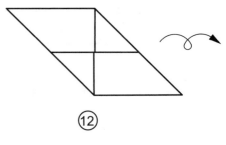

⑫

Turn over.

SONOBE CUBE

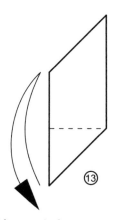

⑬

Fold lower left corner to upper left corner and unfold.

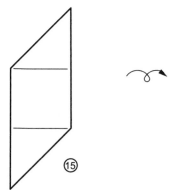

⑮

Turn over.

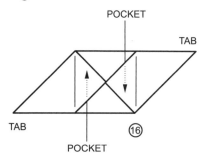

⑭

Fold upper right corner to lower right corner and unfold.

POCKET
TAB
TAB
POCKET
⑯

Completed module. Make 6.

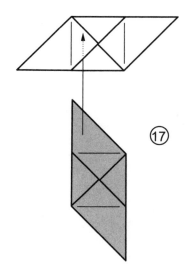

⑰

Insert tab of second module into pocket of first module.

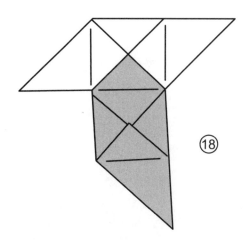

⑱

Complete.

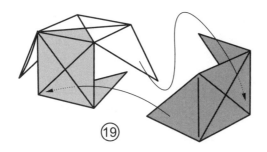

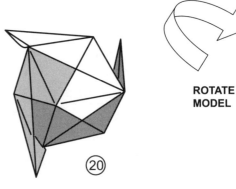

ROTATE MODEL

(19)

The third module completes one corner of the cube by connecting to each of the first two modules.

(20)

Step 19 complete.

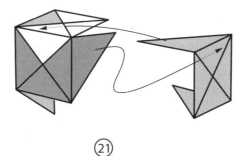

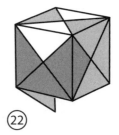

(21)

The next piece is placed opposite the other piece of the same color. Each new piece must complete a corner of the cube by attaching to two existing pieces

(22)

Attach the fifth piece by following the instructions of step 21. This piece will complete two corners of the cube, one corner at a time.

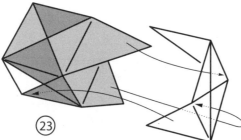

(23)

After the fifth piece has been attached, there will be only one open face remaining on the cube. There will also be two tabs on the cube on two opposite edges of the open face. Place the last piece under and between these two tabs. The last piece will form the remaining four corners of the cube, as it covers the open face.

(24)

Completed Sonobe Cube.

TILE CUBE
Traditional

The Tile Cube is made from six square tiles, connected by twelve square connectors. Each tile is made from two 2 x 1 rectangles, and each connector is half the size of the 2 x 1 rectangle used to make the tiles. All the pieces needed to make one cube can be made from nine squares as follows: cut six of the squares in half to make twelve 2 x 1 rectangles; then cut each of the remaining three squares into four half-size squares to make the twelve connectors.

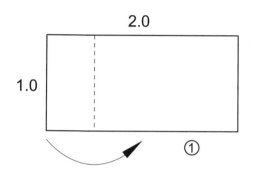

2.0

1.0

①

Fold the left edge to somewhere near the center, making the upper and lower edges line up. You could pinch a crease on the upper or lower edge to mark the exact center, or you could make a mark with a pen or pencil, by eye, to approximately locate the center, or you could estimate by eye when the folded portion is approximately half the width of the unfolded single-layer portion, or when the unfolded single-layer portion appears to be a square.

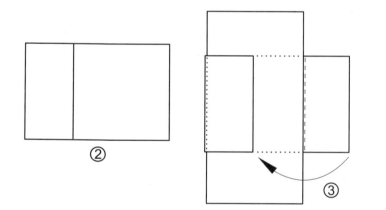

②

③

Place a second rectangle with its long edges vertical under the folded portion of the first rectangle. Place the second rectangle snugly against the crease in the first rectangle. Wrap the short right edge of the first rectangle around the long right edge of the second rectangle.

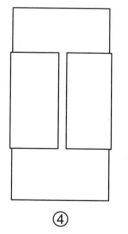

④

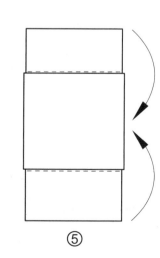

⑤

Turn the model over. Wrap the second rectangle forward around the first rectangle.

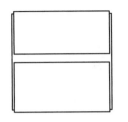

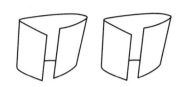

⑥

Separate the two modules.

⑦

Turn one module so its creases are horizontal. Then turn it so its cupboard-door folds face the other module.

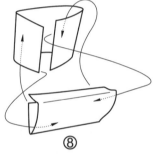

⑧

Join the modules by placing the cupboard-doors of each module inside the cupboard-doors of the other.

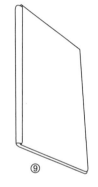

Two cupboard-door folded modules have been assembled to form one square tile. Note that there is an opening on each edge into which a connector may be inserted.

Make six tiles.

⑨

CONNECTOR:

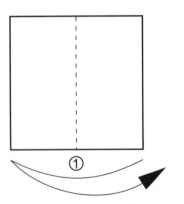

①

Make one crease in the center of the connector. Make twelve connectors.

ASSEMBLY:

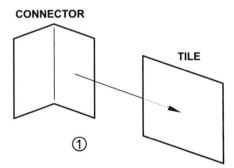

CONNECTOR

TILE

①

Insert a connector into the opening in the edge of a tile, until the crease in the center of the connector touches the edge of the tile.

TILE CUBE

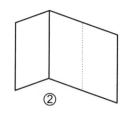

②

A connector has been inserted into the first tile.

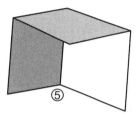

③

Grasp and squeeze the first tile at the location shown by the heavy circle, and insert the exposed end of the connector into the opening in the edge of the second tile until the two tiles touch.

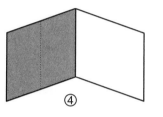

④

Two tiles have been connected. One-half of the connector has been inserted into each tile.

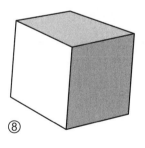

⑤

Add a third tile, making two connections: one between the third and first tiles, and one between the third and second tiles. At each connection, first insert the connector half-way into one tile, then insert the other half into the other tile.

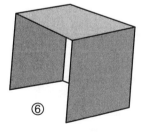

⑥

Next add a fourth tile, opposite the second tile, and the same color as the second. Two more connections are needed to add the fourth tile.

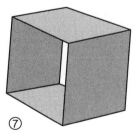

⑦

Add a bottom tile, the same color as the top tile. Three connections are needed to add the bottom tile.

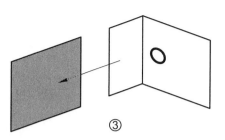

⑧

Add the last tile opposite the first tile. Make it the same color as the first tile. Four connections are needed to add the last tile.

CUBE WITH WINDOWS
Simplification of Lewis Simon's "Decoration Box".
by Bennett Arnstein

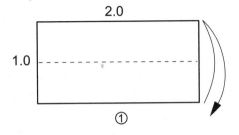

①

Start with a two by one rectangle, long edge on top. Fold the bottom edge to the top edge and unfold.

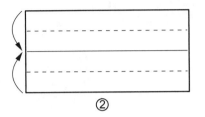

②

Fold the top and bottom edges to the center crease.

③

Module after step 2.

Module viewed from side.

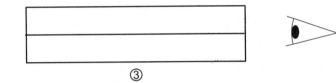

③

Module after step 2. Turn it over.

④

Fold the lower left corner to the upper folded edge.

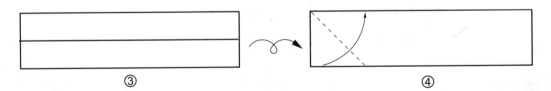

⑤

Module after step 4. Rotate model 180 degrees.

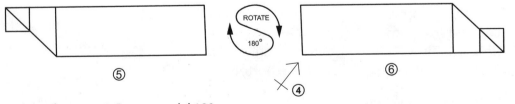

ROTATE
180°

④

⑥

Repeat step 4 on the lower left corner.

CUBE WITH WINDOWS

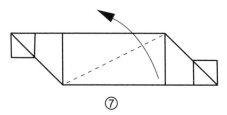

⑦

The crease line runs from the corner on the lower edge to the corner on the upper edge.

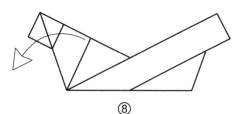

⑧

Unfold the crease made in step 6.

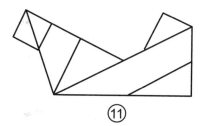

⑨

Fold the lower left corner and edge to the diagonal folded edge.

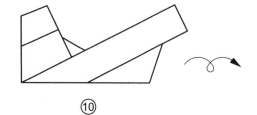

⑩

Turn the module over.

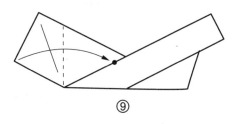

⑪

Repeat steps 8 - 10 at the left end of the module.

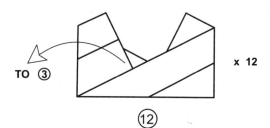

TO ③

x 12

⑫

The module is finished. Unfold to step 3. Make twelve modules.

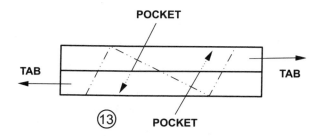

POCKET

TAB

TAB

⑬

POCKET

Note tabs and pockets on finished module.

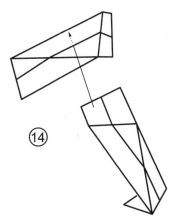

⑭

Connect two modules by partially closing the mountain creases to right angles, and inserting a tab on the second module into a pocket on the first module.

CUBE WITH WINDOWS

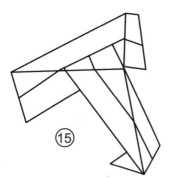

(15)

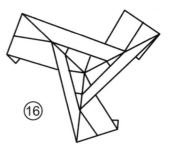

(16)

Two modules have been connected.
The short crease on the entering module
lines up with the long crease on the
receiving module.

Three modules have been connected.
A tab on the third is inserted into a pocket
on the second, and a tab on the first is
inserted into a pocket on the third.

This forms one corner of the cube.

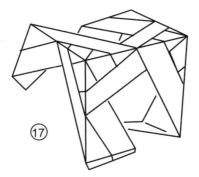

(17)

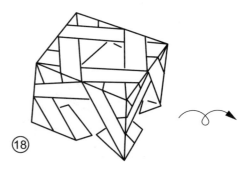

(18)

Add two more modules to the end of one of
the first three modules to form a second
corner of the cube. Always complete a
3-module corner after it has been started
because the three modules hold themselves
together.

Continue adding modules to the
built-up assembly, forming one corner of
the cube at a time, until one face of the
cube has been completed. Then turn the
assembly upside-down with the
completed face on the bottom.

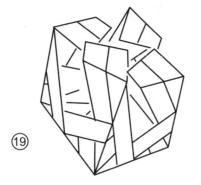

(19)

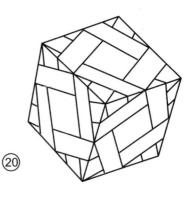

(20)

The Cube with Windows is finished.

With the completed face on the bottom
finish the remaining four corners, one
corner at a time.

26

TETRAHEDRA

SIMPLE CHAIN-OF-4-EQUILATERAL-TRIANGLES FROM A SQUARE
by Lewis Simon .

Makes a two-piece tetrahedron using one LH module and one RH module. No lock tab is needed for this model. To make other models use a CO4ET module with lock tabs, fold it from a 2 x 1 rectangle.

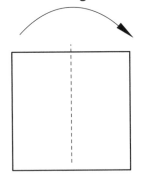

①

Fold the left edge to the right edge.

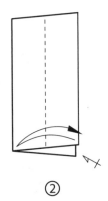

②

Fold the top right edge to the left folded edge. Fold the bottom right edge behind to the left folded edge

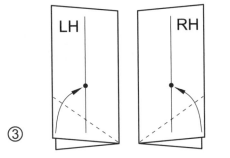

③

Make a left-hand and right-hand module. Fold the top layer only. At each step the modules are mirror images.

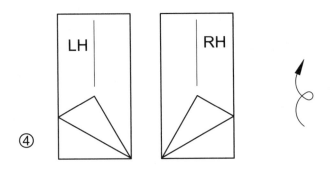

④

Step 3 done. Turn the model over.

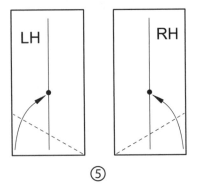

⑤

Crease the top layer only.

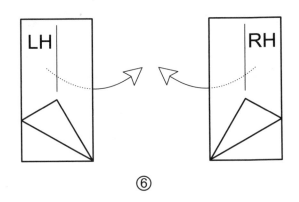

⑥

Unfold the bottom layer.

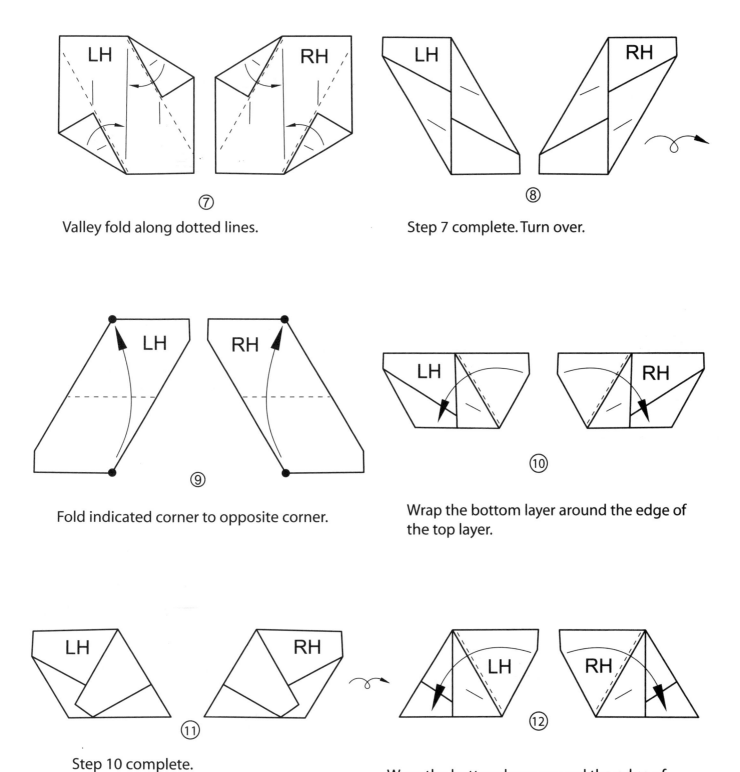

⑦

Valley fold along dotted lines.

⑧

Step 7 complete. Turn over.

⑨

Fold indicated corner to opposite corner.

⑩

Wrap the bottom layer around the edge of the top layer.

⑪

Step 10 complete.

⑫

Wrap the bottom layer around the edge of the top layer.

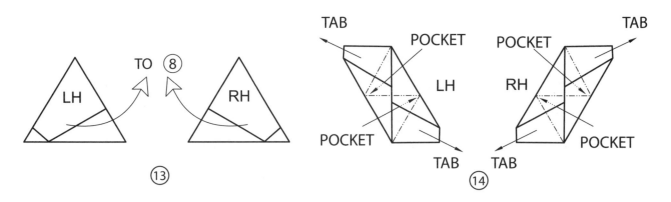

Unfold to step 8.

Note tabs and pockets.

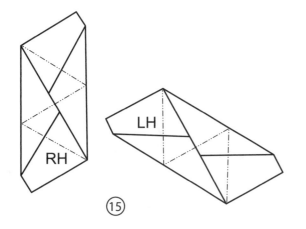

To make a tetrahedron start with one left-hand and one right-hand module as shown.

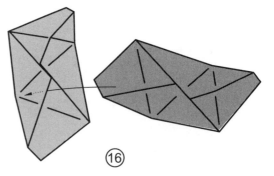

Insert the tab of the left-hand module into the lower pocket of the right-hand module.

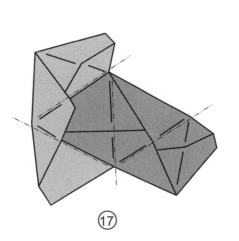

Step 16 complete.

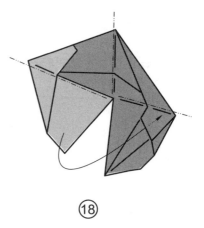

Wrap the left-hand module towards the right-hand one.

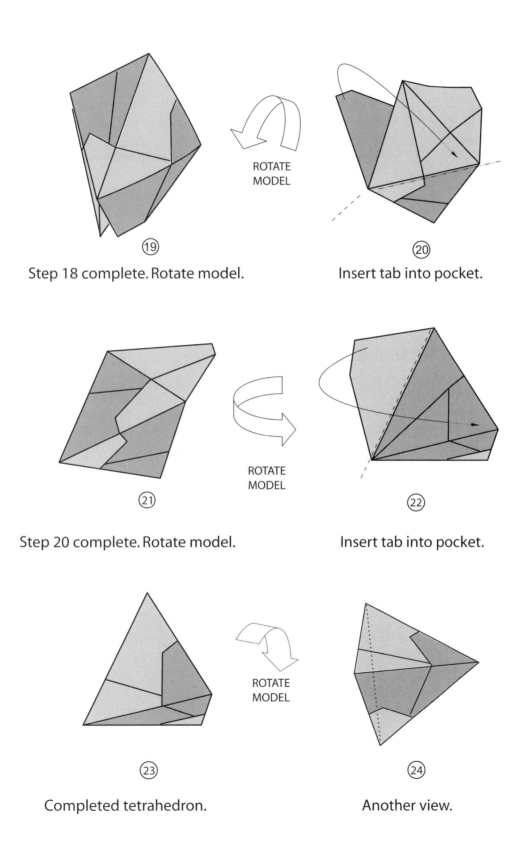

⑲

Step 18 complete. Rotate model.

ROTATE MODEL

⑳

Insert tab into pocket.

㉑

Step 20 complete. Rotate model.

ROTATE MODEL

㉒

Insert tab into pocket.

㉓

Completed tetrahedron.

ROTATE MODEL

㉔

Another view.

EQUILATERAL TRIANGLE MODULE FROM HEXAGON
by Rona Gurkewitz and Bennett Arnstein

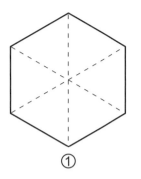

①

Crease all three diagonals of a hexagon.

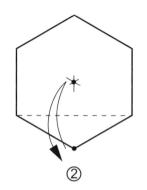

②

Fold the bottom corner to the center and unfold.

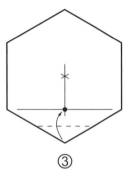

③

Fold the corner up to the crease of step 2.

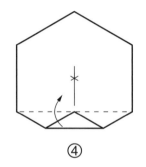

④

Refold the crease of step 2.

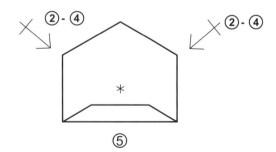

⑤

Repeat steps 2 - 4 at the corners indicated.

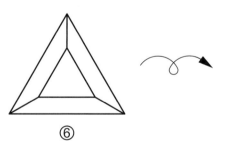

⑥

Turn the model over.

EQUILATERAL TRIANGLE MODULE FROM HEXAGON

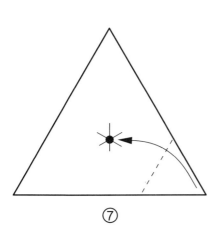

⑦

Fold a corner to center of triangle.

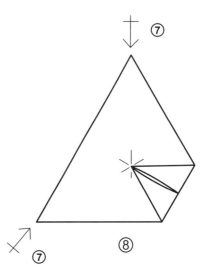

⑦

⑦

⑧

Repeat step 7 at the other two corners.

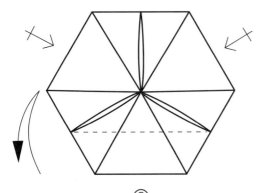

⑨

Fold the bottom edge to the center, creasing through all layers. Partially unfold.
Repeat at the other two sides indicated.

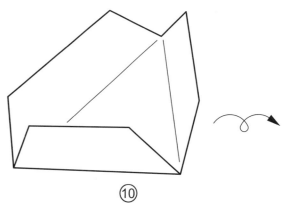

⑩

The module is finished. Turn it over.

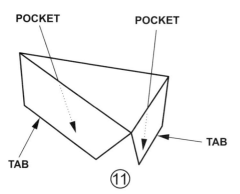

POCKET   POCKET

TAB

TAB

⑪

Each module has three tabs and three pockets. Each pocket is inside a tab.

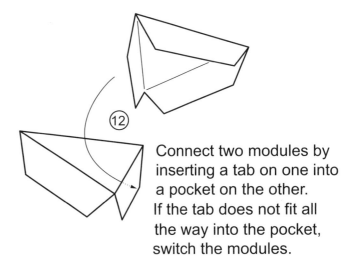

⑫

Connect two modules by inserting a tab on one into a pocket on the other. If the tab does not fit all the way into the pocket, switch the modules.

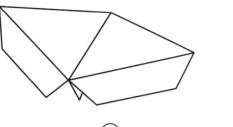

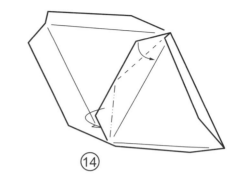

⑬

Two modules have been connected.
Turn them over.

⑭

To lock the connection, fold one corner
of the tab forward and the other corner
backward.

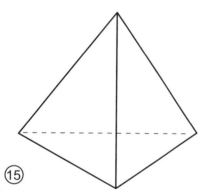

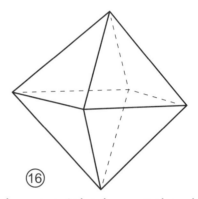

⑮

To make a tetrahedron, make four modules
and assemble with three modules meeting at
each corner.

⑯

To make an octahedron, make eight
modules and assemble with four modules
meeting at each corner.

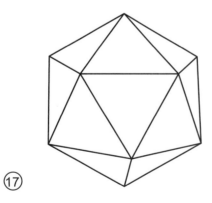

⑰

To make an icosahedron, make twenty modules
and assemble with five modules meeting at each
corner.

EQUILATERAL TRIANGLE EDGE MODULE
by Lewis Simon and Bennett Arnstein

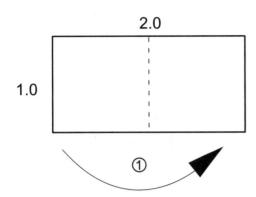

2.0

1.0

①

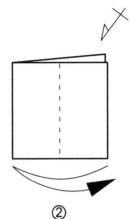

②

Start with a 2 by 1, (half square). Fold the left short edge to the right short edge.

Fold the top right edge to the folded left edge. Unfold.

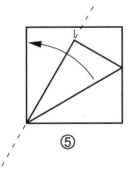

③

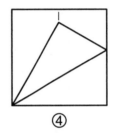

④

On the top layer only, make a crease that passes through the lower left corner, and makes the lower right corner touch the crease in the center.

Step 3 complete.

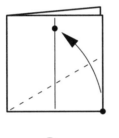

⑤

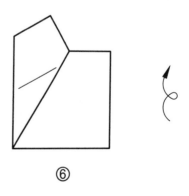

⑥

On the top layer only, fold the lower folded edge up against the left folded edge.

Turn the model over.

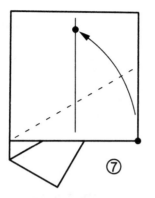

⑦

Repeat step 3

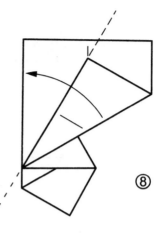

⑧

Repeat step 5.

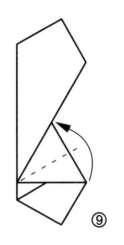

⑨

Fold the right short folded edge
in half.

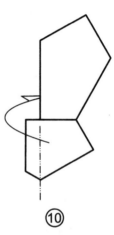

⑩

Wrap the top layer around the
edge of the bottom layer.

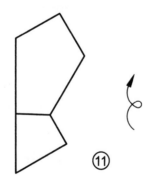

⑪

Turn the model over.

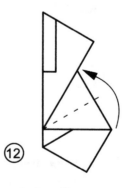

⑫

Repeat step 9.

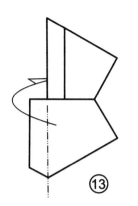

(13)

(14)

Wrap the top layer around the edge of the bottom layer.

The module is finished. Unfold to step 9 and then unfold the bottom layer.

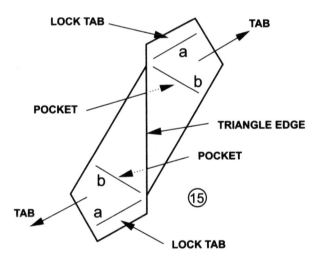

LOCK TAB

TAB

a

b

POCKET

TRIANGLE EDGE

POCKET

b

(15)

TAB

a

LOCK TAB

Note parts of the module.

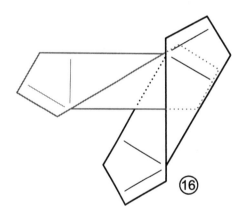

(16)

This shows a gray-line module inserted into a black-line module. Crease a on the entering module lines up with crease b on the receiving module. Crease b on the entering module lines up with the edge of the pocket on the receiving module. If the lock tab on the entering module cannot be used, fold it flat against the tab before inserting the tab into the pocket.

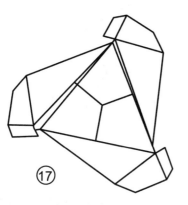

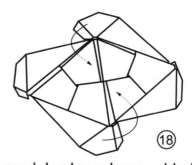

Three modules have been connected to form a triangular face, ready to be connected to another triangular face.

Two modules have been added to the assembly of step 17 to form a second triangular face attached to the first. A tetrahedron has 4 faces with 3 meeting at each vertex. Insert a tab from each face into the other to start a third face at each vertex. Fold each lock tab flat against its tab because the dihedral angles are too sharp to bend the lock tabs around crease b of the receiving module.

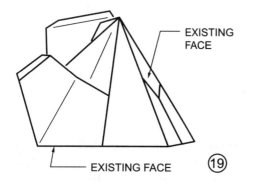

EXISTING FACE

EXISTING FACE ⑲

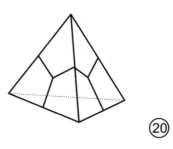

Each end of the sixth module will go into a pocket on one of the existing faces. Each of the existing tabs will go into one end of the sixth module. All the remaining lock tabs should be folded flat against their tabs.

The sixth module completes the tetrahedron.

OCTAHEDRA

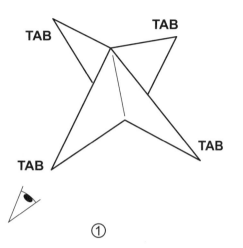

①

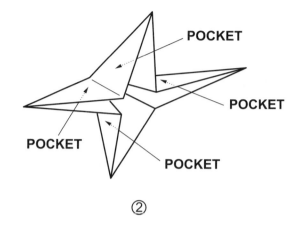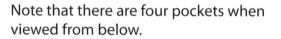

②

Start with a waterbomb base. Note that it has four tabs when viewed on top.

Note that there are four pockets when viewed from below.

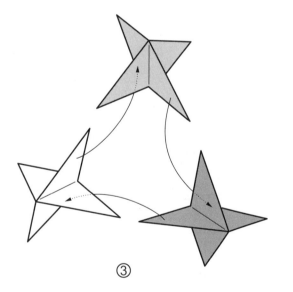

③

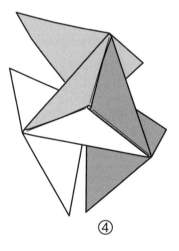

④

Assemble three waterbomb bases of different colors in a ring. Put a tab of the first module into a pocket of the second; a tab of the second module into a pocket of the third and a tab of the third module into a pocket of the first.

This is how the model appears after step 3.

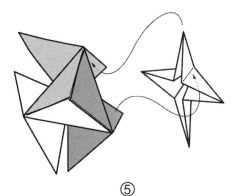

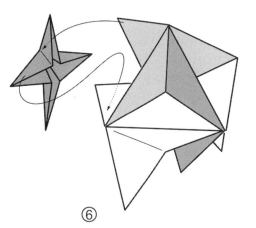

⑤

Insert tabs of model into pocket of fourth module. Insert adjacent tab of fourth module into adjacent pocket of model.

⑥

Add on the fifth module the same way.

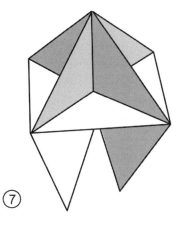

⑦

Five modules assembled. Two free tabs and two free pockets at bottom of model. Add the sixth module to the bottom of the model.

⑧

Insert tabs of model into pockets of module. This is the hardest step. You may have to loosen up the model to get this last module started and then gently ease it into place.

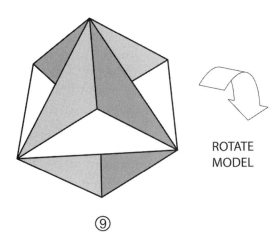

⑨

ROTATE MODEL

Front view of completed model.

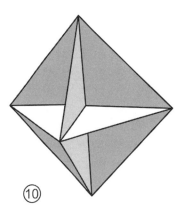

⑩

Another view of completed model.

GYROSCOPE
by Lewis Simon

Assembled from six 2-piece modules.

Made from twelve squares of the same size.

This model is called a gyroscope because you can support it at two opposite corners, one in each hand, and blow on it to make it spin. At step 13 you can measure the size of the cube-shaped opening in the center, and then build a cube to fit in the opening, and place it in the opening before the sixth module is added in step 14.

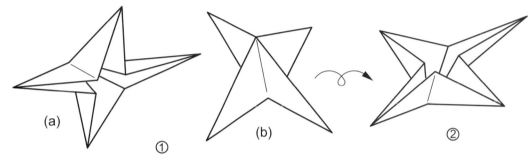

(a)   ①   (b)   ②

Start with steps 8 & 9 of the waterbomb base (page 7). Position (b) will be turned inside-out. Start by turning it upside-down.

Push the center point up, and the model will snap into a new shape, known as the "preliminary base".

③

This is a preliminary base. It is a waterbomb base turned inside-out.

Each 2-piece module is made from one preliminary base and one waterbomb base. Place the preliminary base on top of and outside the water-bomb base. Each corner of the preliminary base goes between two corners of the waterbomb base.

④

⑤

Bring the two pieces together until the centers touch.

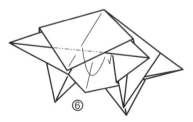

⑥

Straighten one edge of the waterbomb base and wrap the corner of the preliminary base around it. Repeat at the other three edges of the waterbomb base.

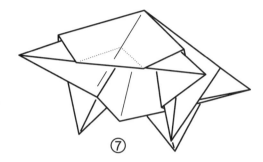

⑦

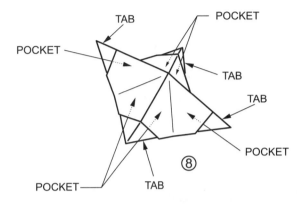

⑧

Repeat step 6 at the other three edges of the waterbomb base.

The 2-piece module is finished. It's shape is a waterbomb base, with four pockets created by the preliminary base wrapped around it.

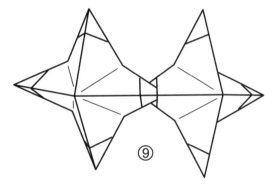

⑨

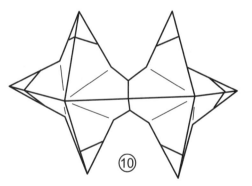

⑩

Connect two modules by inserting a tab on one into a pocket on the other. The entering tab covers the receiving tab.

Push the two modules together until the preliminary bases touch.

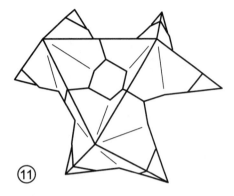

⑪

Add a third module to form a three-sided open space by connecting to each of the first two modules.

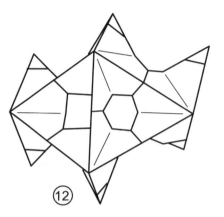

⑫

Add a fourth module to form another three-sided open space by connecting to two existing modules.

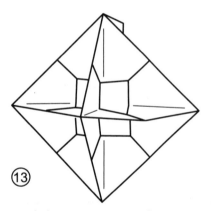

⑬

The fifth module connects to three existing modules, and forms two more open three-sided spaces.

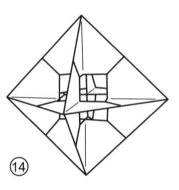

⑭

The sixth module connects to four existing modules and forms four more 3-sided open spaces. The gyroscope is completed.

EQUILATERAL TRIANGLE MODULE FROM HEXAGON
by Rona Gurkewitz and Bennett Arnstein

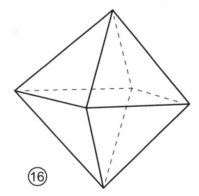

⑯

To make an octahedron, make eight modules and assemble with four modules meeting at each corner. See module instructions in Tetrahedra section (pages 32-34).

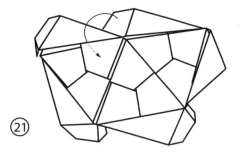

(21)

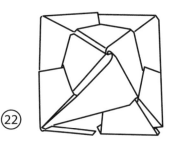

(22)

Add two modules to the assembly of step 18 of the tetrahedron (page 38) to form a third triangular face. Make sure the third face shares a vertex in common with the first two faces, since the goal in making an octahedron is to form a four-sided pyramid at each vertex. Start the fourth face by inserting a tab on the third face into a pocket on the first face.

Use the lock tabs on each unmated tab as a temporary lock to hold the pieces together. Fold each lock tab flat against its tab, and sharpen crease b on each tab to secure the entering module. Now add one module to finish the fourth face, which completes the four-sided pyramid at one vertex.

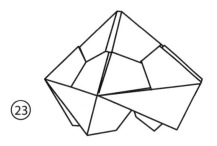

(23)

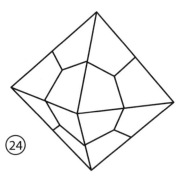

(24)

Continue making four-sided pyramids at each vertex by first making three complete triangular faces and then starting the fourth face by inserting a tab from the third face into the first face. Then complete the fourth face by adding one module. The twelfth module will complete the last two faces.

Try to use as many lock tabs as you can by letting each lock tab bend around crease b on the receiving module. If the dihedral angle is too sharp to allow this to happen, fold the lock tab flat against its tab and don't use it. This completes the octahedron.

108 DEGREE MODULE

independently by Robert Neale and Lewis Simon

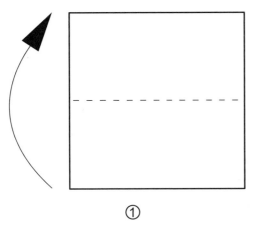

①

Fold the bottom edge of the square to the top edge.

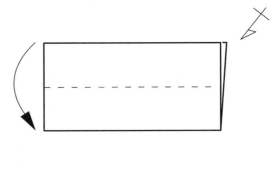

②

Fold the top layer only, top edge to bottom. Turn over and repeat.

③

Module is like an accordion, or the letter M.

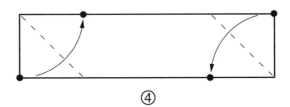

④

Crease through all four layers at each end.

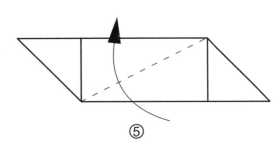

⑤

Crease through all four layers.

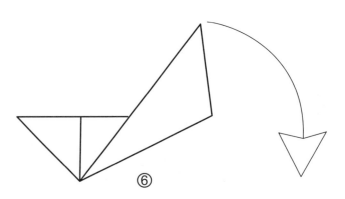

⑥

Unfold to step 4.

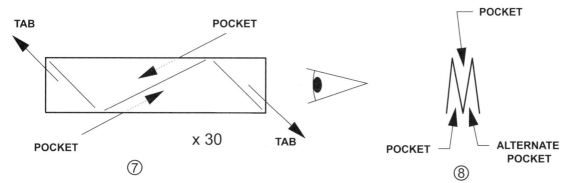

⑦

Module is complete. Make 30.

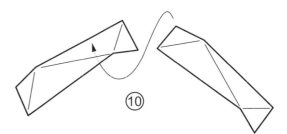

⑧

You need only two pockets on each module. Three are available. Use one pocket on each side of the module when assembling the model.

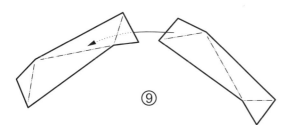

⑨

To assemble the modules, turn them over so the mountain creases face up. The mountain creases face the outside of the dodecahedron ball. Slide one module into the other so the short crease on the tab lies along the long crease of the pocket.

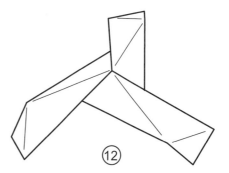

⑩

Alternatively, the tab may be inserted sideways into the pocket. The end result in step 11 is the same: the short crease on the tab lies along the long crease in the pocket, and the two long creases touch at their ends.

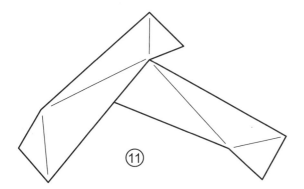

⑪

Two modules have been assembled.

⑫

Three modules have been assembled to form one corner of the dodecahedron. Each module has a tab in the pocket of one module, and a tab from another module in its pocket.

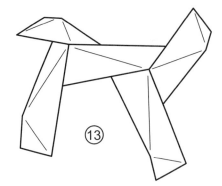

Add two modules to the end of one of the first three modules, forming another corner of the dodecahedron.

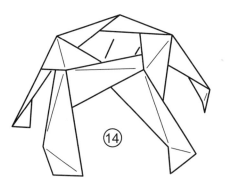

Always finish a 3-module corner before proceeding elsewhere. Continue until a five-sided open space has been completed. Then complete three 5-sided open spaces that meet at one corner.

Continue following steps 9 through 14 until all thirty modules have been assembled. That will complete the dodecahedron. A good coloring uses six colors so no two edges of the same color touch. It is a puzzle, but possible, to use only three colors this way.

TWO-PIECE TRIANGLE GYROSCOPE MODULE
by Lewis Simon

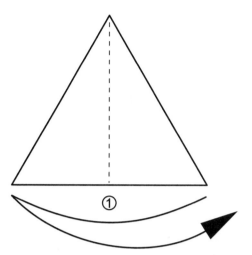

①

Fold one corner of a triangle on top of another. Unfold.

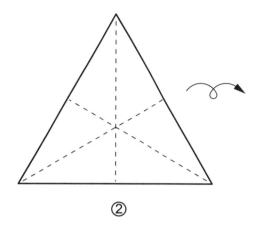

②

Repeat at the other two corners. Then turn the model over.

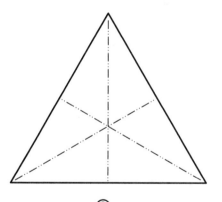

③

The creases are mountains on this side.

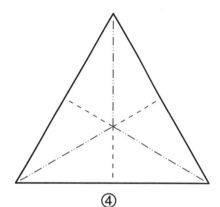

④

Change the creases to valleys between the center and the sides.

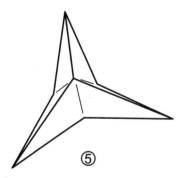

⑤

The model can now form this 3-dimensional shape, called a triangular waterbomb base.

⑥

Turn over step 5 and push up on the center. The model snaps into this shape, which is called a triangular preliminary base. This is step 5 turned inside-out.

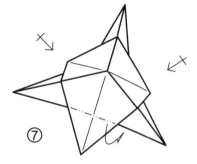

⑦

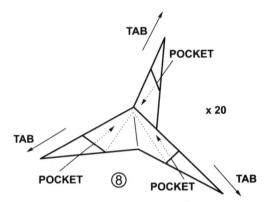

⑧

To make the two pieces make one module, fold one triangle through step 5, and fold the other one through step 6.   Place the preliminary base on top of the waterbomb base, and wrap the corners of the preliminary base around the sides of the waterbomb base.

The two pieces have been joined to form one module. The corners of the preliminary base reach almost to the center of the waterbomb base on the inside.
Make 20 modules to make a dodecahedron.

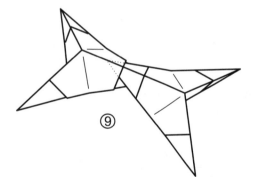

⑨

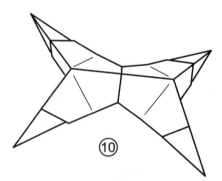

⑩

To connect two modules, the tab of the entering module straddles the tab of the receiving module, and the mountain creases line up. Push the modules together until the preliminary bases touch.

Two modules have been connected.

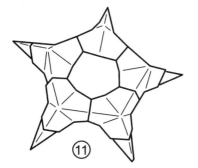

(11)

Add three more modules to form a five-sided ring with an open space in the center. The fifth module is connected to the first module to close the ring.

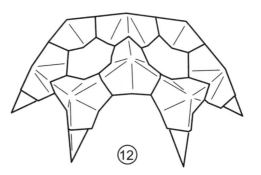

(12)

Add three more modules to form a second five-sided ring attached to the first.

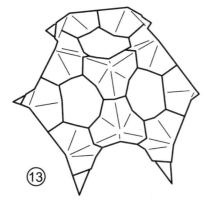

(13)

Add two more modules to complete a third five-sided ring. The three rings meet at a corner of the dodecahedron.

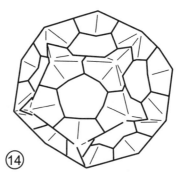

(14)

Continue adding modules to the built-up assembly, first completing 5-sided rings, then making three rings meet at each corner of the dodecahedron. Each module forms one corner. When 20 modules have been assembled into twelve 5-sided rings, the dodecahedron is finished.

DIMPLED DODECAHEDRON
Model by Rona Gurkewitz
Module by Lewis Simon
Connector by Rona Gurkewitz

Five modules are joined to make a 5-sided pyramid.   Twelve pyramids make a dodeca-hedron. The pyramids are assembled using 30 connectors with 3 surrounding a point.

MODULE:

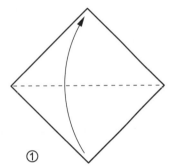

①

Start with a square. Fold bottom point to top.

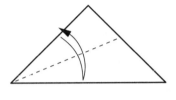

②

Fold the top layer left edge to the bottom edge and unfold.

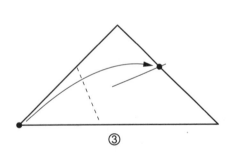

③

Fold left point to right edge where the crease made in step 2 ends.

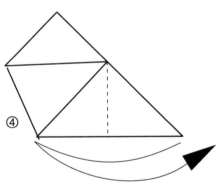

④

Fold the right bottom point to the left bottom point and unfold.

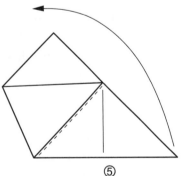

⑤

Wrap the bottom layer around the edge of the top layer.

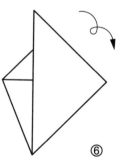

⑥

Turn the model over.

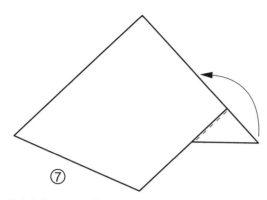

⑦

Fold the small triangle over the edge.

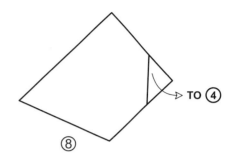

⑧ → TO ④

Unfold to step 4.

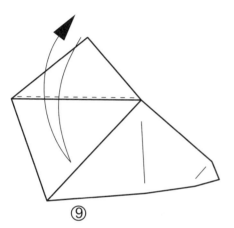

⑨

Wrap and unwrap both bottom layers around the edge of the top layer.

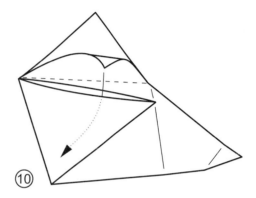

⑩

Insert the top right-angle corner on the bottom layer into the pocket, folding along the crease of step 9.

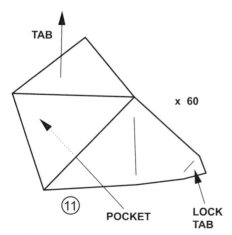

TAB

x 60

⑪

POCKET   LOCK TAB

The module is completed. Make sixty. Twelve of five colors each is good.

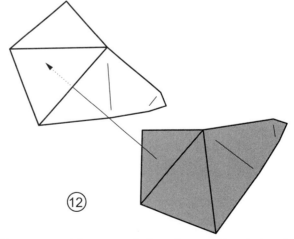

⑫

To connect two modules, insert the tab of the second module into the pocket of the first.

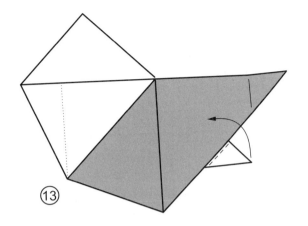

⑬

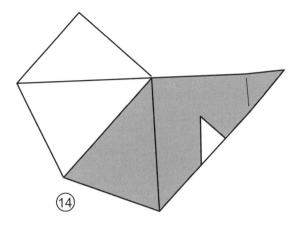

⑭

With the second module fully inserted into the first, wrap the lock tab of the first module around the edge of the second.

Two modules have been connected and locked. Continue adding modules until five modules have been connected. Then connect the first module to the fifth, forming a five-sided pyramid. You will have to move the fourth module forward to connect the fifth module.

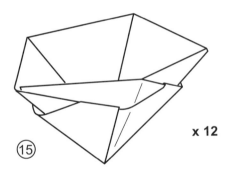

x 12

⑮

CONNECTOR:

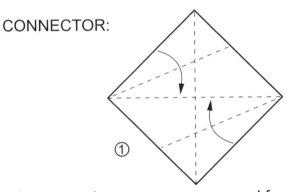

①

Five modules have been assembled to form a 5-sided pyramid. Make 12 pyramids.

Use the same size square as was used for the module. Crease the square along both diagonals. Fold the upper left edge and the lower right edge to the horizontal diagonal.

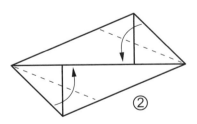

②

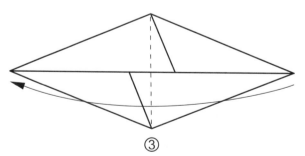

③

Fold the short left and right edge to the center horizontal line.

Fold the connector in half. The crease coincides with the existing crease on the bottom layer. This completes the connector. Make 30.

DIMPLED DODECAHEDRON

ASSEMBLY:

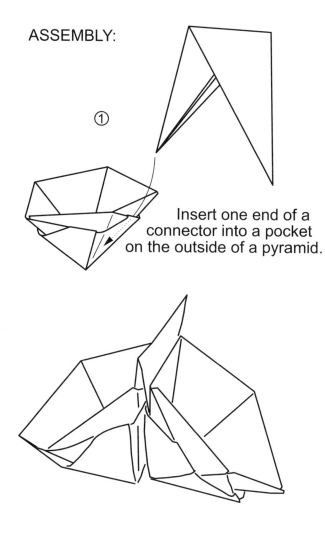

① Insert one end of a connector into a pocket on the outside of a pyramid.

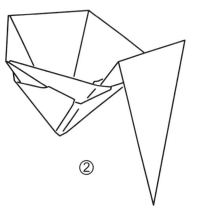

② Push the connector all the way into the pocket. Then insert the other end of the connector into a pocket on a second pyramid.

③ Two pyramids have been connected by one connector. Every connector connects two pyramids.

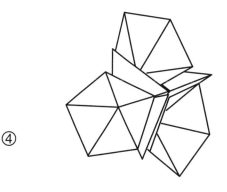

④ Three pyramids have been connected with three connectors. One connector connects the second and third pyramids, and one connector connects the first and third pyramids. Three pyramids meet at each corner of the dodecahedron.

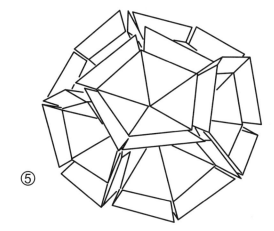

⑤ Continue adding one pyramid at a time to the built-up assembly, making each new pyramid form a three-pyramid corner with two existing pyramids. Continue until one of the three original pyramids has been surrounded by five pyramids. When all twelve pyramids have been assembled, each one will be surrounded by five others.

ICOSAHEDRA

EQUILATERAL TRIANGLE MODULE FROM HEXAGON
by Rona Gurkewitz and Bennett Arnstein

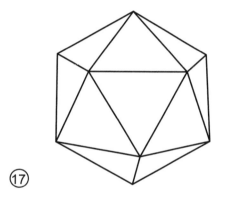

⑰

To make an icosahedron, make twenty modules
and assemble with five modules meeting at each
corner. See module instructions in section on
Tetrahedra (pages 32-34).

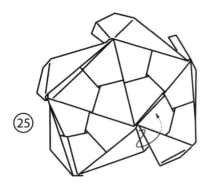

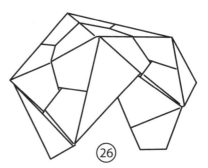

Add two modules to the assembly of step 21 of the octahedron (page 46) to make 4 triangle faces meeting at a vertex. Insert a tab from the fourth face into a pocket on the first face to start the fifth face. Every vertex of an icosahedron is formed by a five-sided pyramid.

Add one more module to finish the fifth face of the first 5-sided pyramid.

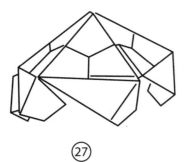

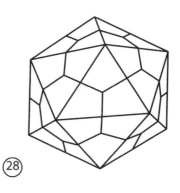

This completes the first 5-sided pyramid. Continue adding modules to make a 5-sided pyramid at each vertex.

Be sure to use the lock tabs to form temporary locks to keep the modules from coming apart, as explained in step 22 (page 46). The thirtieth module will finish the last two faces to complete the icosahedron. All the lock tabs will be used because the dihedral angle between the faces is open wide enough to allow the lock tabs to bend around crease b on the receiving module.